The Shadow of My Porch Swing

Stories of God's Presence

Volume 1

Shauna Thomas

Cover Art and Sketches: Shauna Thomas
Photo of Author: Sunny Thomas

The days ebb and flow,
Swing to and fro,
But God always remains
He is with you today

CONTENTS

INTRODUCTION

I grew up in South Louisiana where the days are muggy and the mosquitos are abundant. On a dead-end street, named after my family, in the middle of town, I was related to most every person on that strip of asphalt. Small towns have their pros and cons but the best part is the community. I loved our porch. It was the door of invitation, a safe place to watch the world change and the epicenter of communication. As I've grown up, moved and occupied many different residences, there has always remained a deep desire to sit a spell on the porch with a tall glass of tea.

My current place in life has a porch swing that has become my safe place. As a wife and mom of four miracle boys, the sounds of chaos can quickly overtake my thoughts. I have found my sanity on that swing numerous times. I choose to break away, readjust my attitude and pray…lots of prayers.

I sit there in a sundress in a warm summer breeze. I comfort a crying child that has a rough day. I laugh or grieve with friends and bundle up in blankets while the wind strips the trees bare or snow blankets the ground. While the seasons always change, the one thing that does not change is the swing's shadow. Sometimes when it's really faint, I'll flip on the porch light just to see it better.

And that's how I have learned to meet God on that swing. Whether the pendulum of life is on the upswing or I'm experiencing the drop in my stomach going down, Jesus is always there.
He is present in the wild rides or the stationary silence.
All I have to do is join Him and sit a spell.

There is an old saying 'the shadow proves the sunshine.'
My prayer is that even if you can't seem to find the Son,
His shadow will prove He hasn't gone anywhere.

PAUSE IN GOD'S PRESENCE

As you journey through this devotional, you will find daily scriptures, some reflection questions and a prayer. I have shared stories from my life in hopes that you can relate now and then to how God shows up in all the small places, calm or crazy alike.

The use of the word **Selah** traces back to the original Hebrew Bible where it is most often used in the Psalms. The full meaning is unknown although most agree it is a term of **pause**. A breath or stop from what has come before and preparation for what is coming next.

As you read through each day, my prayer is that you would pause at the end to hear God's sweet voice spoken to you. This is not a checklist or guilt trip. It is an invitation to meet with the One who is waiting for you.

I've included some of my sketches from my personal journals throughout the pages. Space has been provided each day for your own notes, drawings or journaling as you begin to see the presence of God with you daily. Embrace the swing of life and watch your story unfold.

WHAT DID YOU SAY?

But don't just listen to God's word.
You must do what it says. James 1:22a

Jesus answered, "Everyone who drinks this water will be
thirsty again, but whoever drinks the water I give them
will never thirst. Indeed, the water I give them will
become in them a spring of water welling up to
eternal life." John 4:13-14 NIV

Often in life, I have moments where I don't hear something clearly. Usually it's with a family member and my imagination tends to jump to the negative. What did they say? I can't believe that. Do they really think that? I even do it with God. I'll hear a sermon, podcast or speaker and if I get distracted I think "What? Really? Is that what God really says?" The temptation often is to file it away and accept the more 'educated person's statement' instead of reading the Bible for myself.

Currently, my days are still filled with a little sidekick who needs me to read signs for him. Today at the museum, we were standing by a new hands-free water fountain that didn't have buttons. As we try (and fail) to get it to turn on, I tell Nathan, "No you don't have to push the circle, it's hands free." He promptly responds, "Maybe it's hands four" and holds up four fingers in front of it. I chuckle at his statement and stoop closer to his ear to read the sign to him again. For him, free equals three and he can't read, so he misheard and therefore misunderstood the directions.

The same goes with God. It is important to be in the Word for myself, not just hearing it from other sources. When I invest in face-to-face time with God's truth, read and understand the very directions He has set out for me, then my actions can be effective and produce life-giving water.

**Have you ever wondered, "Did God really say that?"
Even Satan posed that very same question to Eve in the
Garden of Eden. Take time right now to study some Bible verses
regarding your questions.**

Father, You promise that when I seek You, I will find You. Today as I bring my doubts or concerns to You, lead me to the truth. Speak clearly to my heart where I can understand. I know You are trustworthy and Your words refresh my soul and give me life.

_____

_____

_____

_____

_____

_____

_____

_____

YOU ARE MY FATHER

All praise to God, the Father of our Lord Jesus Christ, who has blessed us with every spiritual blessing in the heavenly realms because we are united with Christ.
Ephesians 1:3

Where can I go from your Spirit? Where can I flee from your presence? If I go up to the heavens, you are there; if I make my bed in the depths, you are there. If I rise on the wings of the dawn, if I settle on the far side of the sea, even there your hand will guide me, your right hand will hold me fast. Psalm 139:7-10 NIV

Our boys are great holiday car travelers. Not many incidents of "are we there yet?" or "I need to go potty!" The kids mostly read or play 'I Spy' and as long as I keep to the snack schedule, it's a pretty quiet ride. The peace of our last holiday trip to a theme park was surprisingly interrupted an hour into the drive by the wail of our six-year old crying, "I want to go to Branson!" Matter-of-factly without turning around I respond, "Well, it's a good thing you boarded the right train. This one is headed to Branson."

Now my husband is a whole other personality, fun and witty...probably because he gets more sleep. So Chris dramatically announces, "OH NO! We forgot your ticket. We have to stop. We need to kick you out."

GASP! Now it's vital for you to know that this was spoken to the most emotional and tenderhearted child on this planet. Fully expecting tears, I quickly turn around to ward off the flood but instead I'm greeted with a giant toothy smile and nugget of truth.

"No, you don't have to kick me out cause you are my father. I get to go with you," he confidently states.

God often has a way of using my sons to speak the very truth I need to hear. Because I have a personal relationship with Jesus, I have the privilege of being a child of God. No matter what happens, I always get to go where my Father goes.

What makes you feel unworthy to go with God today?

Father, remind me that I am Your child and You delight in traveling with me. Help me have confidence to know You will never kick me out of Your presence.

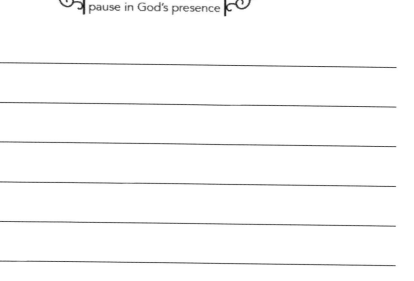

_____

_____

_____

_____

_____

_____

_____

_____

GLORIOUS CREATION

He determines the number of the stars and calls them each by name. Psalm 147:4 NIV

When I look at the night sky and see the work of your fingers—the moon and the stars you set in place— what are mere mortals that you should think about them, human beings that you should care for them? Psalm 8:3-4

Leaving Carlsbad Caverns, New Mexico, after the evening bat flight, we detour at the entrance along the road. This is our last stop during a full week of traveling National Parks of the Southwest. With a new moon, anticipated Orionid meteor shower and a view from horizon to horizon, we can not help but take a moment to reflect on all we have seen. Tallest peaks, largest forests, unique cultures, biggest cities, grandest canyons, longest caverns; it has been a week filled with the extraordinary…and this last view doesn't disappoint.

Tracing the white streak of the Milky Way across the sky with my hand, the boys look and experience the vastness of the heavens. Words fail until a falling star breaks the silence. Our regularly viewed constellations are lost among the visual noise of a billion new lights surrounding them. My boys ask all their names and I can only answer with the truth. "I don't know. But God knows every one, and yet He knows you too. You are thought of with more care than any star and He chose to reveal His love to you. He thinks you are greater and more magnificent than anything we have seen this week and He wants to have a relationship with you."

My mind drifts to a familiar song and I begin to hum aloud.

And as You speak
A hundred billion galaxies are born
In the vapor of Your breath the planets form
If the stars were made to worship so will I
I can see Your heart in everything You've made
Every burning star
A signal fire of grace
If creation sings Your praises so will I
(Hillsong UNITED/ So Will I)

And so I realize the sum of our trip is a worship song that turns my eyes and heart to the Creator of it all. I have nothing to offer, yet He offers me this journey. A chance to travel down the road of life, explore the unknown, trust Him as provider, seek wisdom for which path to take and how to guide our boys, and at the end of it all, stand speechless before His majesty.

Who am I that You are mindful of me?

If creation sings Your praises...so will I.

Have you stood in awe of God's greatness lately? Take time to check out the stars tonight or look deeply at something you love and praise the Lord for His majesty.

Father, Your creation is astounding. So intricately detailed yet incomprehensible at the same time. You existed before and without it, yet You created this world so that I could know You, understand Your character and stand in awe before You. I was the 'why' and reason You spoke life into this world. In Your eyes, I shine brighter than any star. Here I am in awe of You.

DESERT

But then I will win her back once again. I will lead her into the desert and speak tenderly to her there.
Hosea 2:14

When the poor and needy search for water and there is none, and their tongues are parched from thirst, then I, the Lord, will answer them. I, the God of Israel, will never abandon them. I will open up rivers for them on the high plateaus. I will give them fountains of water in the valleys. I will fill the desert with pools of water. Rivers fed by springs will flow across the parched ground.
Isaiah 41:17-18

Pulling out of the driveway, I sigh and wish he would trust me. Unwillingly he had slumped into the house, unhappy and discontent. Without a hug goodbye or a look, he curled up on the couch and buried his head under the blanket. He had wanted to go to the other house and play video games with his brothers. He despises being alone or feeling left in the desert, but his heart is hurting. I saw it in his eyes this morning when he got up and heard it in his voice all day as he found reason after reason to fight my love.

As a parent, we often find ourselves caught between what our child wants and what they need and the clash of those titans can feel like WW3. He just wanted to lose himself in a video game but I know he needs some one-on-one time so I led him to the best place I know for that, alone at his Nana's house.

God has a great plan for this boy but it looks so different from the rest. Most see the struggle but Nana sees the spectacular. I know she loves him extravagantly, looks for the extraordinary and speaks value

17

into the deepest parts of his heart that even I overlook which is exactly why I brought him here. To his desert. Alone. Because of love.

God is a good father and often does the same thing to me and, admittedly, I fight the process too. I'm an extrovert, give me people and parties and more things to occupy my mind. It's easy to think escape and fulfillment is found in some made up reality full of time spent playing the game of life I want. Instead, He takes my hand and leads me away. He says 'trust me, I know what you need, what your heart truly wants. It might seem like you are being left alone, separated from what you love but I'm separating you for love. A chance to meet your heart at its lonely and broken place and offer you quality time with one who gives you extravagant love.'

A few hours pass and a picture flashes on my phone. Bright shining eyes and a true smile, one I don't see often, but that I know lies within. Met inside with music he loves and tender words, he ditched the blanket as she took him on an adventure where his heart (and belly) were fed to overflowing.

Being alone is not what I want and I definitely don't know it is what I need right now, but I find myself led here to the desert anyway with a choice: embrace the one-on-one or bury my head. If I will just look up, I will see the desert isn't empty nothingness; it's where Jesus wants to fill up all my empty places to overflowing.

Go with Him today. Do you trust God to lead you and fill you?

Father, being led into a desert is different than being abandoned. I go willingly with You today. Help me hear Your tender voice, fall in love with You and allow You to fill up all my empty, dry places.

SELAH
pause in God's presence

he is FAITHFUL

A CASE OF THE GROSSIES

Create in me a clean heart, O God. Renew a loyal spirit within me. Psalm 51:10

My van is lived in, seriously. At any given moment you could probably find a full set of clothes and enough food scraps to last you a day or two. It's not that we spend a ton of time in the van, it's more that my boys are lazy and don't take out what they daily put in.

Today, as I was ritualistically deep cleaning in preparation for a trip, I discarded an entire trash can of grossness while saving a laundry basket full of items needing to go back inside. Good news, I found the (renewed-5 times-to avoid a fine) library book. Bad news, I became even more aware that one child has a hoarding problem. If ever in a bind, he could stuff a shirt with saved used tissues and have a really nice pillow.

While cringing (and gagging) at the state of his little domain, I became acutely aware that my life is often in the same shape. A lot of junk brought or let into my heart that I refuse to deal with or take back out. Just shove it under the seat, it will eventually disintegrate, right? May I be willing to dive in, clean out the grossness and breathe deep knowing I can start my next journey clean, without taking along the trash from the last one.

What have you been holding on to that needs to go in the trash?

Father, give me the desire to expose my heart to Your light. Show me what needs to be cleaned up so that I can be renewed with Your truth.

SELAH
pause in God's presence

GREEDY GUS

"Consider carefully what you hear," he continued. "With the measure you use, it will be measured to you— and even more." Mark 4:24 NIV

The sun is up and it is time to wake the sleeping bears. I have a love/hate relationship with mornings. I love standing in my boys' room staring at all their sweet sleeping faces (yes, they all share one room.) However, I hate waking them up. How such a sweet face can morph into such immediate nastiness is a direct result of low blood sugar levels. I've suggested a solution to my husband, but it's tricky. If we could just insert a feeding tube while they are sleeping and give them breakfast round one, I'm fairly confident that we could conquer breakfast round two without missiles flying.

Our kitchen is the perfect boxing ring because one particular Big bear lives and breathes in the realm of 'fair'...well, as long as 'fair' favors him, if you get my drift.

Yesterday, he walked into the kitchen while brother was pouring cereal. A LOT of cereal. I wasn't surprised because this brother always eats the most, but the world ended for Big bear. Tears appeared and accusations began to fly. "He is greedy! His bowl has too much! It's all the way full! He only thinks of himself! Greedy, greedy!" Quietly, I walk over and pour half the amount for Bigs. I guess I must have stepped on his toe because his wails grow louder.

"That's not enough. My bowl is only half full! You are unfair!"

Now surely you can understand why I'm completely baffled and confused at this last retort and a conversation ensues.

"Well, I don't want you to be accused of being greedy, since you are so upset about your brother's bowl."

The sharp reply comes, "That's not greedy, that's fair!"

"Well son...if it's fair and he is greedy then that makes you greedy too." Silence follows.

I wish I could say the lesson was learned, apologies given and we've all learned to give each other grace in the mornings. I can only say it's all a work in progress. Me included. I find myself in just as many 'fair fights' mentally as I experience verbally with my kids. I do it at work, in school, at the grocery store, and most often sitting in church.

Why is it OK to hold others to a different standard than I hold myself? Where can you grow in generosity?

Lord, may I be aware of the hidden judgments in my heart. Give me a heart of generosity in all things. A desire to think the best, assume the best and act in the best interest of others.

SELAH
pause in God's presence

_____

_____

_____

_____

_____

_____

IMMUNE

Therefore, I urge you, brothers and sisters, in view of God's mercy, to offer your bodies as a living sacrifice, holy and pleasing to God—this is your true and proper worship. Do not conform to the pattern of this world, but be transformed by the renewing of your mind. Then you will be able to test and approve what God's will is—his good, pleasing and perfect will. Romans 12:1-2 NIV

Do you not know that your bodies are temples of the Holy Spirit, who is in you, whom you have received from God? You are not your own; you were bought at a price. Therefore honor God with your bodies.
1 Corinthians 6:19-20 NIV

Sitting and waiting for longer than usual in the hospital pharmacy, my youngest son found a flavored tongue depressor under a chair...and licked it. Yes! In the most germ-riddled place where everyone carrying every kind of disease congregates, the lure of the sweet smell on a fancy, bright red, animal topped stick sucked him in. Tongue and all. I almost puked while his big eyes searched mine trying to figure out why I was so upset.

A few days passed as I kept an eagle eye on him but he didn't get sick. He obviously had enough antibodies to fight off the germs and I was astounded at his immune system.

Often when we have sat in the world long enough something allures us, draws us in and we consume it. The smell, the taste, the glitz and thrill of the find. We know better but we just can't resist. Just like my son experienced, those around us might be appalled and horrified. They gag and puke at the thought of our actions while we stare on, wondering what is the problem. If we have been consuming the world long enough, this is not a new fight. We might not even get sick. We have become immune to the ingestion of those germs.

24

Yet the Bible states that our bodies are the temple of the Holy Spirit. Instead of focusing on not getting sick, let us choose instead to ingest holiness.

In what area of your life are you willingly ingesting sin or unhealthy things?

Father, give me eyes to see with clarity all that I desire to consume. Make me aware of things I am putting in my life that are not good for me. Give me strength to admit my choices and a desire to choose holiness instead.

_____

_____

_____

_____

_____

_____

_____

_____

DIRT AND WORMS

Is anyone thirsty? Come and drink— even if you have no money! Come, take your choice of wine or milk— it's all free! Why spend your money on food that does not give you strength? Why pay for food that does you no good? Listen to me, and you will eat what is good. You will enjoy the finest food. Isaiah 55:1-2

I'm familiar with the five love languages but am convinced that food most definitely is number six. Fortunately, I grew up in the Deep South where eating well was not a problem, even for us poor folk. I'm pretty sure I could happily survive on beans, cornbread, rice, and gravy for the rest of my life. Simple is good. Now that I have five boys in the house, I'm convinced that food can solve any problem. Sick? Chicken and dumplings. Mad? Ice cream. Big game? Pretzels and crackers. Tired? Grilled cheese and apples.

If I notice they have had a rather hard work or school day, my favorite quick go-to is pudding pie. Just a simple box of pudding poured into a graham cracker crust. It takes all shapes. Lemon and cream, vanilla and bananas, chocolate and cookie crumbles. Add some gummy worms, give it a cool name and we are rocking the party! My family gathers around the table quickly when I call. They come empty handed and leave filled up. It's my joy to feed them because I love them.

Today Jesus invited me to come to His table. Come and eat, He wants to fill me up, yet I have this lingering doubt. Do you really want just me? I don't have much to offer...I should really bring something...earn my place at your table. I scrape together a chocolate dirt and worms pudding pie full of excuses, I'm sorrys and should haves. I bring along a list of what I think I got right and how I'm trying so hard. It's the best I could do amidst the hurriedness of life.

Arriving, I'm embarrassed to see I am His only guest. There is a table full of my favorites laid out before me as a reminder of how well He knows my heart. Then Jesus himself serves me. The main course of truth with a side of grace and oh-so-sweet bread of life lathered in love. I set my dirt and worms pie off to the side realizing my effort wasn't needed, He just wanted me to enjoy dinner on the house.

What makes you hesitant to come empty handed before God? What truth do you need to consume today?

Father, Your table is lavish and Your love is extravagant. You freely gave Your Son for my life so I know You will withhold nothing less. I want to enjoy the finest food, not settle for leftovers. Help me have ears to hear Your call so I can quickly come eat at your table.

SELAH
pause in God's presence

POTTY MOUTHS

May the words of my mouth and the meditation of my heart, be pleasing to you Lord. Psalm 19:14

If you can't be kind, be quiet. That laminated, large, printed statement holds permanent residence in our boys' bathroom. It's truly amazing how many unkind words can come out of one bathroom of boys, four boys at that. Growing up as an only child, I never shared a bathroom. I didn't know the woes to be had when someone filled the toothpaste tube with water or soaped the handles or spit on an arm or (gasp) didn't flush their poop. The state of their bathroom often pales in comparison to the state of their halitosis filled mouths. Oh, how they need daily mouthwash, both externally and internally. If I'm really honest, they are not the only ones needing a clean mouth.

All too often, I let the hurried responsibilities of life or the troubles of those around me taint my heart. It skews my thoughts and my words follow suit. The mess gets made and then the poop of the mouth gets left unflushed; bringing unpleasantness to all who share my space.

The antidote we have found is THANKFULNESS. Thinking kind and thankful thoughts leads to speaking kind and thankful words. So, everyday we take a few minutes of our morning to say three things we are thankful for out loud. The mornings of quiet have become mornings of encouragement. Try it. Three thankfuls, or more, if you really need a good cleaning. I promise it doesn't burn as much as mouthwash.

What area of your speech needs a good cleaning? Are you argumentative, boastful, critical or a naysayer? Ask God to grow a spirit of thankfulness in word and action. Spend time listing things you are thankful for today.

28

Father, remind me that You are always with me and always listening. May the words I say and the thoughts I think be pleasing to You.

THINGS I'M THANKFUL FOR:

ENOUGH EXPECTATIONS

*My flesh and my heart may fail, but God is the strength of
my heart and my portion forever. Psalm 73:26 NIV*

*Each time he said, "My grace is all you need. My power
works best in weakness." 2 Corinthians 12:9*

*And you will know the truth, and the truth will set
you free. John 8:32*

Tonight didn't quite go as planned. My day started well; off to
church, lunch and cleaning, painting delivered and a long menu of
items readied for the big game. I love hosting people, especially our
family nights. I am not the best 'party planner' and I usually forget
something important like drinks or silverware but my heart overflows
with a house full.

While I embrace the chaos that comes with adding others to our
space, I have learned to anticipate some typical reactions. I know that
two of my boys will immediately lose their minds. All calm and sense
will fly out the door as they seek every bit of family attention and
begin running their very own circus. Another one will retreat to
imagination world...and be adamant that I am the only one that can
come along to play, and the oldest will immerse himself right in with
the adults.

When all gears are running on high, I find myself managing chaos,
and enjoying it for the most part. My expectations line up with reality
so there isn't much of a rub. There is a kink tonight though: I'm not
running 100% healthy and I forgot to clean the bathroom. After
remedying the latter and knowing there is a 1:1 ratio of children to

family members in the next room, I linger in my room, hoping to steal some minutes to myself. Just a short breather and a prayer to feel better. I sure do not enjoy feeling sick.

The silence is broken by a second set of expectations: his disappointed voice asking why I'm not engaging in the party or watching the game. His heart just wants me with him but I hear accusation instead. While a very loud voice of reason wants to 'tell it like it is,' I stuff it and rejoin the group instead. However, before I can see one game play on television, I'm redirected by my small circus to our playroom. Cars racing around, Legos under foot and a game of catch ensue. Three smiling faces happy for my undivided attention, or what they can see of it at least. As I sit, my mind replays the lie over and over. "You're not enough. You failed. You slacker." And so I give more. Smile more. Play more. Hug more. Fix more. Clean more. All while the lie plays on.

Quietly reflecting on tonight in the silence that now hangs heavy in the house, the tears come as I hear a different voice. "I AM enough." HE speaks and my mind stops racing. Enough. It's what Jesus keeps saying to me: to my run-ragged, lie-believing self. It's my word for this year and proving to be a big learning curve. I haven't learned to dwell there yet, though I expect I will often have reason to do so. God loves like that, not giving up until we give in.

The still small voice is followed by a loving, familiar voice asking for my forgiveness. Not just apologizing, but listening and grieving with me over the lies that have wrecked my soul. So we both learned at the party tonight that those expectations are powerful weapons. Opening doors for truth or lies. But in the end, I get to decide what stays for the after-party and tonight it is *Enough*.

Have you ever let false expectations weigh heavy on your heart? What would it take for you to reject the lie and believe God's truth instead? Where do you need to admit 'I am not' so that God can show you He is 'I AM'?

Father, there are so many moments where I believe a lie instead of truth. Thank You for being enough for me every time I feel like a failure. I don't want to be chained to false expectations. Teach me Your truth so that I can be set free.

SELAH
pause in God's presence

_____

_____

_____

_____

_____

_____

_____

_____

_____

PRAYER PROBLEMS

But Moses pleaded with the Lord, "O Lord, I'm not very good with words. I never have been, and I'm not now, even though you have spoken to me. I get tongue-tied, and my words get tangled." Then the Lord asked Moses, "Who makes a person's mouth? Who decides whether people speak or do not speak, hear or do not hear, see or do not see? Is it not I, the Lord? Now go! I will be with you as you speak, and I will instruct you in what to say."
Exodus 4:10-12

Jesus said, "This is how you should pray: "Father, may your name be kept holy. May your Kingdom come soon. Give us each day the food we need, and forgive us our sins, as we forgive those who sin against us. And don't let us yield to temptation." Luke 11:2-4

And the Holy Spirit helps us in our weakness. For example, we don't know what God wants us to pray for. But the Holy Spirit prays for us with groanings that cannot be expressed in words. Romans 8:26

I was trying to pray this morning and kept getting all tripped up. My words and thoughts were a jumbled mess and I felt like I just could not get my act together. Sure, I can talk the hind leg off a horse but praying always seems like such hard work.

This afternoon, I am still sorting through these emotions while I pick up one of my sons from school. As we head to his appointment, I take note that he is being extremely careful with his words. I hear him often start one word but then change that word mid speech.

Knowing exactly why he is fumbling, I turn around after parking and look him in the eyes. "It's obvious you are avoiding words with R's. Please know I am so proud of your effort this past year. Do not be ashamed that it still takes work." He relaxes some and gives me a smile. You see; this crazy gifted, good-at-everything child carries around some kryptonite in the form of a slight speech impediment. But it does not make me love him less or not want to listen to him. Sure, sometimes he does not sound quite like the others and I have to find undivided time each day for his practice, but I never say, "I wish he just wouldn't talk to me." I actually cherish the extra one-on-one face time I get with him.

Tonight, I think God is telling me the same thing as well. It does not matter that I don't get all the words right or that I sound different than those around me. It does not even matter if I tip toe around the hard things in an effort to make it easier on myself. He has already set aside undivided time to listen to me and is proud of how I have grown. He can not wait for me to tell him about my day, even when it takes a little while for it to all make sense. I just have to show up and start talking.

Do you struggle with believing that God is waiting to talk to you? How has the need to 'pray-it-right' stopped you from communicating with your Father?

Jesus, my words are a jumbled mess most of the time. Either tumbling out in excitement, broken up by emotion or clammed up by confusion. What a relief to know that even Your disciples needed help with prayer. When I feel inadequate, help me trust our relationship and talk to You anyway. You delight in hearing my voice.

SELAH
pause in God's presence

_____

_____

_____

_____

_____

_____

_____

_____

_____

_____

_____

_____

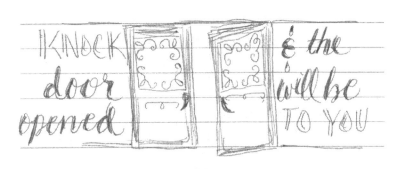

I KNOCK door opened & the will be TO YOU

THE POTTER

We now have this light shining in our hearts, but we ourselves are like fragile clay jars containing this great treasure. This makes it clear that our great power is from God, not from ourselves. 2 Corinthians 4:7

Every year, my family visits an arts and crafts theme park in Missouri called Silver Dollar City. Each time we go, I visit the pottery shop. I am fascinated by the clay, mud, slip, glazes and kiln. Yes, I'm that annoying guest asking questions the whole time the artist is trying to work. Over the years, I have noticed a rhythm to the process and it all starts with a block of clay in a cardboard box. Every beautiful piece in that shop starts with flawed clay. It is full of bubbles, cracks and imperfections. The potter could choose to hastily shape a bowl or mug from a piece of that lump, but it would be destined for the trash. Hidden problems expose themselves once under fire. So as the potter sits and works the clay, folding it, pressing, removing and identifying flaws, it begins to take on a new identity. No longer a flawed lump of clay, it becomes a beautiful piece set aside to dry.

But what happens when a problem arises while drying? A new crack or bubble revealed during isolation. I've learned that it's not too late. Even bone dry pottery can be remade if exposed to a moist environment. Sometimes it's a simple fix; sometimes it becomes an entire reworking from a new inspiration. What was once a bowl, now a mug. A plate is now a pitcher. After glazing and firing, the newly worked piece shines gloriously.

Just like that clay, I am initially full of flaws and not good enough to withstand the refiner's fire. God, my potter, could leave me as is but instead, he draws me up and out. If I am intent on being left alone, untouched and unworked, I am destined for destruction. On the other hand, when I surrender to His merciful hands, he sees my flaws and in love he remakes me, even if I am bone dry. I have a new, useful identity. Reflecting his light and filled with his glory.

2 Corinthians 5:17 confirms this promise from God as Paul speaks truth about being made new. *"This means that anyone who belongs to Christ has become a new person. The old life is gone; a new life has begun!"*

Do you feel too cracked and flawed to be useful? What area of your life do you need to surrender to God to be remade?

Father, thank You for seeing through my flaws and failures and placing Your tender hands on me. I know You will never stop working to make my life into a beautiful, useful vessel. Help me live full of the new life You have given me.

_____

_____

_____

_____

_____

_____

GRACE

Three times I pleaded with the Lord to take it away from me. But he said to me, "My grace is sufficient for you, for my power is made perfect in weakness." Therefore I will boast all the more gladly about my weaknesses, so that Christ's power may rest on me. 2 Corinthians 12:8-9 NIV

But as for me, it is good to be near God. I have made the Sovereign Lord my refuge; I will tell of all your deeds. Psalm 73:28 NIV

Today I'm putting on my big girl pants and going. A week ago I made a call I've dreaded for months. You know exactly what I mean, we have all made one of those calls before...or maybe you're still waiting. Whether it was a doctor call, a relationship call, a job call or a call for help. It's the thing you've put off for days, months or maybe years because you just haven't had the energy to deal with it...and everything you think it brings.

For sixteen years, I've asked the Lord to take it away, and for a long time human efforts have helped but time and pain have finally had their way in wearing me down, so I'm waving my white flag. I surrender. My self-sufficiency is no longer enough so I'm seeking help. This specific trial is physical, but I've seen many a friend endure emotional and spiritual battles that are just as real and cost just as much. The Lord knows I've got a handful of those, too, wrapped up in my roles of wife, mom, sister, daughter and friend.

As I read this morning that His grace is sufficient, my heart is a bit distant. In the church world, I often hear that grace is 'getting what you don't deserve' and when I think about my salvation, absolutely! My sinful self deserves none of God's favor. But today, in this trial, I honestly can't help but think 'I sure am getting something I don't deserve, and there is nothing pleasant about it…how is that grace?' Off I go to the dictionary. Grace: unmerited divine assistance. Ok, that helps. When I can't do anything about this situation, God's assistance is enough. I'm glad to read on that his power is made perfect in weakness because I identify with that part. Remember that white flag?

While I have been dreading this day, I stop to take a breath and remember that for the last sixteen years the Lord has been near. He has always opened doors for me to speak of his goodness in this (and many other) less than good situations. I know that he will give me the same divine assistance today if I call on him. I made the first call already, the next one should be easy. I think I'll change my slogan from putting on my big girl pants to putting on his big God power.

In what situation do you need God's power to assist you? Is it hard to admit that you are weak and need help? Ask today.

Father, Your grace is sufficient. Your assistance is enough. It's okay that I can't handle this on my own. You know it's good for me to stay near You but I often use my own strength to fight through this life. Thank You for making me weak today so I can have Your power instead. I can't wait to tell others about our adventure together.

WAITING

You will keep in perfect peace those whose minds are steadfast, because they trust in you. Isaiah 26:3 NIV

Sixteen years ago I had an assignment to take one Bible verse, study it and write a message. I vividly remember squatting against a wall in silence for a minute before I started my speech yet it felt like 10,000 minutes. I had chosen Isaiah 26:3 because after three failed surgeries the previous year, I was currently in a season of waiting.

As a habitual doer and go-getter, waiting still comes with great effort. Over the years I've found I repeat this verse to myself almost weekly. Waiting for a job, waiting for a good doctor's report, waiting for a home to open up in another state while driving there in the moving truck, waiting years to get pregnant, waiting eighty-five days in a hospital bed once I was pregnant, waiting for the right counselor to help us, waiting for relationships to be reconciled, and lots of waiting for prayers big and small to be answered.

I wish I could say that I have learned to wait well and that it comes easy but I would be lying. This morning I am faced with waiting again. In addition to four upcoming surgeon appointments and several unknowns weighing on my mind, we currently wait daily to see if the teacher strike will be over tomorrow and our kids can return to school.

The enemy wants me to waiver and get overwhelmed with uncertainty during the ebb and flow of my days. How thankful I am that God's Word is alive and active. Because I have hidden His word in my heart, I take a deep breath and remain steadfast. He is with me and promises His perfect peace even in this season of waiting. He never failed me then and He won't start today.

**What are you waiting for God to do in your life?
Are you choosing to remain steadfast and trust Him
even when you don't see results?**

*Father, thank You for never playing hide-and-seek with me. I can
have Your peace; and You tell me exactly how to get it. Help me
remain steadfast in Your truth and trust that You are with me in the
wait.*

SELAH
pause in God's presence

_____

_____

_____

_____

_____

_____

_____

_____

_____

_____

_____

I AM NOT ALONE

The LORD himself goes before you and will be with you; he will never leave you nor forsake you. Do not be afraid; do not be discouraged. Deuteronomy 31:8 NIV

A time is coming and in fact has come when you will be scattered, each to your own home. You will leave me all alone. Yet I am not alone, for my Father is with me. John 16:32 NIV

I'm am not alone. I am not alone. You will go before me, you will never leave me. That worship song by Kari Jobe runs thru my head every single time I need to pee. I just want to be alone. For 30 seconds. A minute would be heavenly. Please!

If you have ever been a parent or even watched kids for awhile, I'm sure you understand. I am convinced there is a silent alarm set across the door of my bathroom. It could have been silent in the house for thirty minutes or more. Everyone working on projects, playing or reading but the moment I walk in the bathroom...Mom, where are you? I need you. Mom, can you look at this? Mom, he touched me. Mom, who was the first person to split an atom? I am an extrovert by nature, I love being around people. Before kids on a personality scale of 1 being introverted and 10 being extroverted, I ranked a 10. The last time I took this test I ranked a 5. I contribute the decline completely to ten years of bathroom intrusions.

As I read through the Bible, I see a constant push and pull between 'please don't leave me' and 'I need some space.' Even Jesus lived and spoke of this tension. When He was tired and needed to be refreshed, He would often go away by himself to a hilltop or quiet place to pray. He even invited those in His presence to do the same. In Mark 6:31, Jesus is very direct as He says to his disciples, "Come with me by yourselves to a quiet place and get some rest." However, He also showed compassion and sacrificial love when He met large crowds who had followed Him after He tried to find some privacy. (Matt 14:13-14)

Jesus knows what it is like to be constantly needed. Clothes tugged on and requests asked of Him day and night. Even healing power taken from Him by surprise. I love our real-life Bible sharing how the disciples went ahead for food while Jesus sat down at a well alone. He was plumb worn out and knows how it feels to need a break.

Through the everyday ups and downs, our human bucket gets filled and poured out. Sometimes we need more filling and sometimes we overflow. Sometimes we want out of a relationship, sometimes we are hurt that those relationships are gone. In John 16, Jesus speaks to the disciples the truth that they will all leave Him. The very ones who have been all up in His business for over 1,000 days are going to run away and leave Him alone. These are the guys He wants by His side in the garden in His final hours. He doesn't want to be alone, but He finishes with, "yet I am not alone, for my Father is with me." If you have ever been or are currently in a situation where you feel completely alone and don't like it, Jesus understands that too.

I'm still learning to embrace the tension of being needed and needing to recharge. I believe our flesh battles it all our life. First wanting a break while caring for those around you and then missing that season when they are no longer there. In the moments where I look up and my heart skips a beat because no one is around, my spirit overflows with joy that I am never really alone. The Lord goes before me and He will never leave me.

Are you needing to get away and find rest today or do you need to ask others to come alongside you? What truth of God's never-leaving presence do you need to embrace?

Father, thank You for understanding my real-life struggles. Sometimes I need rest and a chance to recharge and that's okay. Help me embrace interruptions of these times with compassion and love. Other times, I need support around me but don't find what I need and feel alone. Fill my mind and heart with truth that even then, I am not really alone. You are always with me.

SELAH
pause in God's presence

GOD WITH US

BURNED

No. No. NO! I did it again. While I love to cook and for the most part can successfully get a complete meal to the table, I am notorious for burning something. Usually, it's the bread. But if it's not the bread, it's something in my skillet. You know the one, your favorite non-stick skillet that cooks everything perfectly. Yep, that one. This time I got distracted (surprise, surprise) by some small ones arguing and I ran back to the kitchen to smoke and a black skillet. WAH!

That was three days ago. The skillet is still soaking in the sink. Everyday I scrub a little more until my fingers, wrist and arm get tired or my resolve to clean it diminishes first. I really want my skillet back. How could I have been so careless? It wasn't even on purpose but that five-minute distraction has caused days of frustration and effort to clean up.

I sure wish this wasn't a perfect picture of my faith, but unfortunately it often is. I pull out my faith in Christ and use it to serve me or others and expect everything I encounter in life to just slide right off that non-stick surface. But then it happens, something distracts me and I forget to tend to my faith and sure enough, it gets burned. Let me just check Facebook or Instagram first this morning. Wow, she's got it together and I don't. How could that kid do that? Why am I still dealing with this? All those little distractions take my eyes off of what I am called to focus on and suddenly I find myself left with a charred heart and mess to clean up. A mess that will take ten-times longer to clean than to make.

So now I have a couple of choices. I could just throw away my skillet and go buy a new one. I've known some friends to do that. Throw away their faith because it's too burned and cleaning it up seems too hard. Go find a new church, religion, god or quit looking altogether.

I could pretend it's not a burned mess and keep cooking things right on top. Unfortunately, that keeps leaving this nagging charcoal flavor tinting everything I serve. I wish I didn't know the bitter taste of living with a charred part of my heart still affecting my life, but I do.

Or I can roll up my sleeves and get to work. Scrub a little today until I'm worn out and then work at it again tomorrow. I relate to Paul when he encourages the Philippians to 'continue to work out their salvation with fear and trembling.' I fear seeing that skillet in the sink again today, but ignoring it isn't going to help, so I researched and found a spray that helps eat through the char. Spray, wait and scrub. Spray, wait and scrub. It's almost there. I might even have the resolve to finish it up today if I don't get distracted.

God is speaking to me about my relationship with Him also. It's not just my effort or willpower. When I research in His Word, I'll find truth to spray on those burned spots. Wait for Christ to soften an area and then do the work of scrubbing. It might take some days or months but I'm determined to get it back so I keep at it. Perseverance sure does pay off, because a little more shines through everyday.

Have you given up on a part of your faith or feel like there is just too much of a mess there to ever be useful again? What area is God wanting to soften and restore today?

Father, my heart is often burned by the things of this world and the mess left behind seems insurmountable. Will You come in, speak truth and soften the hardness? I don't want to give up but I need encouragement to persevere. Thank you for the truth that I am worth it and useful. No matter how many burns happen, You keep working on me so I can shine.

_____

_____

_____

_____

_____

_____

GUMMY BEARS

*He chose to give birth to us by giving us his true word.
And we, out of all creation, became his prized possession.*
James 1:18 NLT

Have you ever tried to take gummy bears from a toddler? Well, I have a toddler that is passionate about gummies of all sorts. Sour, sweet, bears, worms and especially those little packages that hang out in our snack bin. I've been finding empty wrappers around the house lately, stuffed behind pillows and even under my bed.

I promise I feed him...All. The. Time.

I caught him in action yesterday morning before my world was up and running. When his eyes met mine every gummy from the package quickly found a hiding place inside his clamped fists. It was amazing really; the speed at which they disappeared. I knew better, he wasn't just going to hand them over but I tried asking anyway. Ha! What was I thinking?

So I did what every good mom does at 7:00 am when your child is opting for candy instead of breakfast nutrition...I tried to open his hand to get them. It was quite hilarious. My effort pitted against the tiny iron fist. The calm with which he stood there, staring, locked down on his prized possession, knowing those gummies weren't going anywhere. I gave up and started laughing as Scripture rushed through my head.

"My Father, who has given them to me, is greater than all; no one can snatch them out of my Father's hand." John 10:29

Just as those gummies found a swift, complete and secure shelter in that fist, so I found an immediate, complete and secure place in God's hand when I chose Jesus as my Savior. And if Jesus is your saving hope, you have the same security. He chose us first, before the world was awakened, and made us His prized possession. Rest secure. You're not going anywhere.

Do you feel safe in your Father's hand today?

Father, thank You that You will never let me go. No matter how hard the world pulls and pries, I cannot be removed from Your hand. Thank You for holding me safe and secure and for making me Your most prized possession.

_____

_____

_____

_____

_____

_____

_____

_____

_____

FOOD COURT FRIENDSHIP

Children are a gift from the Lord; they are a reward from him. Children born to a young man are like arrows in a warrior's hands. How joyful is the man whose quiver is full of them! Psalm 127:3-5

For everything there is a season, a time for every activity under heaven....A time to cry and a time to laugh. A time to grieve and a time to dance. Ecclesiastes 3:1,4

But Jesus said, "Let the children come to me. Don't stop them! For the Kingdom of Heaven belongs to those who are like these children." Matthew 19:14

To all the people trying to have a nice Friday evening at the food court, I apologize. It was me doubled over in laughter with my friend as our kids raced Nascar-style around us. It was me walking hoards of children up and down the corridor looking for some food joint, any food joint really, that was still open. It was me ignoring the whines, gut punches and falls while the smallest one drank out of every. single. cup. Sure, our planned nice-family-dinner hadn't quite worked out and here all twelve of us sat in a food court in the midst of chaos but I once heard said 'the table doesn't have to be extravagant because the people always are' and it holds exceptionally true tonight.

It's been twelve years since the four of us sat together on couches comforting one another in our season of loneliness. Desiring children yet the medical reality forecasting something completely different. Understanding fully the path we each walked, we prayed, entrusted the future to the Lord, and committed to rejoice with and encourage each other. Years have come and gone. Several states separate us.

Information is shared via blog or online. Christmas cards cross paths, all while prayers remain.

Tonight we are the chaos in your midst. Eight children in six years between us (yes, you read that right), gifted by God as the fulfillment of His promise to provide. Some of these gifts came sooner than later, some from different cities and some as complete surprises but each a unique and tangible mark of God's hand in our midst. And so I laugh and smile (and break for timeouts) and embrace the dirty looks because I am completely enthralled with the presence of my friend. No judgment or comparison between us. Just two moms walking in the grace and love of Jesus, laughing and sharing life...and thankful for husbands who are feeding our circus.

As the ever-moving amoeba of now-best-friends swirls with glee around us, I can't help but feel the smile of my Jesus. "Let the little children come to me," He reminded His closest friends. "The kingdom of God belongs to such as these." They aren't a problem; they are the purpose. You see us sitting in chaos, I see us sitting on couches. Not much has changed really. We still intimately understand this season of life. We still desperately need Jesus to walk us through each day and we still commit to rejoice with and encourage one another.

Who knows what twelve more years will bring? Gray hairs and laughter are a given. Maybe stories of redemption or celebrations of new beginnings. There might be tears of sorrow or frustrations at choices. Whatever that season brings, our friendship will remain...and maybe dinner will be better than a food court.

Who can you encourage today in the midst of their chaos? Do you need encouragement? Pray and ask the Lord to supply your need.

Father, I thank You that You bring along encouragement in my seasons of drought. This life of motherhood hasn't quite worked out like I planned, but You are always faithful. Thank You for reminding me to steward well the gifts of children You have entrusted to me.

SELAH
pause in God's presence

_____

_____

_____

_____

_____

_____

_____

_____

fill me with JOY

BOUNDARY BENEFITS

The boundary lines have fallen for me in pleasant places;
surely I have a delightful inheritance. Psalm 16:6 NIV

If there is one thing that will bring on immediate eye rolling in our house it's a saying I repeat almost daily.

> *When you are somewhere you are not supposed to be,*
> *doing something you are not supposed to be doing,*
> *or with someone you are not supposed to be with,*
> *then you will get a consequence you are not supposed to have.*

Usually every major issue in our house can be boiled down to one of those scenarios. Even today, we have a black fingernail and sad child from playing around with slamming doors. It took everything in me to not say "I told you so."

That specific saying may have come from my mouth but I am most definitely not the author of that truth nor is our family the first to experience it. Almost every tragic Bible story from Adam to Jesus has a main character involved in the 'not supposed tos.' While reading the story of David and Bathsheba the other day, I stopped and actually gasped out loud. There on the page in front of me I saw it: a man somewhere he wasn't supposed to be (at home instead of war), doing something he wasn't supposed to be doing (enjoying the scenery), with someone he wasn't supposed to be with (someone else's wife) and the consequences were great.

Poor choices always affect more than one person. David's sin spilled all over those around him. He lied, made others lie for him, murdered a mother's son, made a wife a widow, betrayed his friend, disgraced the Lord's name, and ultimately grieved his son's birth and subsequent death.

Oh what meaning it brings to David's admission in Psalm 16 when he cries out "The boundary lines have fallen for me in pleasant places; surely I have a delightful inheritance." King David had learned firsthand that just as Jerusalem was safeguarded from the enemy by high walls, his own life was also kept safe within the Lord's boundary lines.

As parents, we pray to raise boys that will grow in wisdom and stature and favor with God and others. Part of gaining wisdom is understanding cause and effect. Sometimes it gets tricky in this sinful world because good choices don't always get the good consequence, however rest assured that bad choices almost always have a bad consequence, often far beyond the scope we envision.

So for now, I continue to recite this truth daily to our boys while our stakes are low. Smashed fingers heal much quicker than shattered hearts and families. As we rapidly approach emotional teenage decision-making and increased eye rolling, I pray God's truth and my voice are a constant nag to be where and with and doing what they are supposed to. It is a joy to live within the boundary. It offers true freedom for your soul.

Remember a time where you wanted to fight against a safe boundary in your life. What was the outcome? What area is God currently asking you to respect?

Father, You are my protector and provider. I know that when I step outside of Your plan that I open myself up for attack. My sinful nature loves to rebel and says freedom comes without restraint. I reject that lie. Teach my heart to trust that true freedom is found within Your secure and loving boundaries.

SELAH
pause in God's presence

_____

_____

_____

_____

_____

_____

_____

_____

_____

_____

_____

_____

_____

_____

_____

SANDING

And we know that God causes everything to work together for the good of those who love God and are called according to his purpose for them. Romans 8:28

I love wood. All shapes and sizes, colors and species. I grew up with scraps of wood laying all around our house, so it wasn't long before I was straightening used nails and building things myself. After I got married, I convinced my husband that he needed a miter saw, then a table saw...and a router...and a planer. I know, I know. I have a problem. It's called splinters.

Whenever we build a piece of furniture, there is a finished product in mind. Unfortunately, it won't get there without some effort and change. Some planning, cutting, gluing and nailing is definitely required. After that it sure looks nice and is functional but it's not useful...remember the splinters? It must be sanded, a lot, with different grits in different ways. Electric sanding gives way to block sanding which gives way to hand sanding. Each step a vital part of the process.

Now I admit, I hate sanding. I can be a little impatient and distracted, often wanting to just *'get 'er done'* and if it is taking too long I may even *'take a break'* and move on to another project. And that's how my garage fills up with half-done projects. As a woodworker, if I really love that piece, I have to finish the process. If I don't sand that table and rid it of splinters, it will sit untouched and useless in the garage.

Lately I've been acutely aware of my own splinters poking out and hurting those around me. A verse, a song, that quiet conviction, a word of correction from a friend...or, heaven forbid, from my husband, I begin to feel God's sandpaper rubbing me. It is then, I have a choice to make. Sit as I am in the garage, or trust that His love wants me to become an exquisite place for others to gather. What do I choose? Surrender to the sanding. I want to be made beautiful and useful.

Is it easier to ignore your rough spots or to admit you need work? What is keeping you from trusting God that this sanding is for your good?

Father, it is so hard to endure the rub of correction. Help me trust that You are smoothing out my rough edges for my good and for Your glory. As others spend time with me, let me be a safe place to gather, not one covered in splinters.

SELAH
pause in God's presence

_____

_____

_____

_____

_____

_____

_____

CAR WASH

For they don't understand God's way of making people right with himself. Refusing to accept God's way, they cling to their own way of getting right with God by trying to keep the law. For Christ has already accomplished the purpose for which the law was given. As a result, all who believe in him are made right with God. Romans 10:3-4

I wish I was one of those people that love washing. Any kind of washing really: dishes, clothes, self...it's a wet/dry thing; trust me. Vehicles are the worst. The blowing dust, dirt roads and winter ice melt all make for a nice hazy sheen that regularly adorns my van. Summer is great because I recruit the boys to soak it down and scrub, but otherwise it's too cold and I can't trust them to not soak each other.

So now it's really bad. After months of procrastination, I head to an automatic car wash, pay, pull through the line and am stopped by the attendant. Sitting at the starting block watching the corridor of swirling motion ahead feels like waiting to walk into Pee Wee's playhouse. Enough of that; focus on the guy waving his hands at me.

This man is an excellent candidate for a charades competition. Pointing and directing, he silently guides me forward. A little left, turn that wheel, up some more...now stop. Then he points to the list of rules: arms inside, windows up, mirrors folded, antenna down, van in neutral. Check, check, ready to go. Not quite. He knocks on my window and points again to the bottom: *hands off the steering wheel.* Now I can go.

As I sit still in my moving car, I'm reminded of Jesus. I drove up to this car wash, paid my dues, listened to the attendant and followed all the rules knowing that the outcome would be a clean van.

However, until I took my hands off the wheel and trusted the tire catch to pull me through, nothing changed.

Same with faith, I can go to church, pay my dues, listen to the pastor and follow all the rules, but that only gets me to the right starting place. I have to let go and give my life over to Jesus to pull me through the wash. What a blessing to come out clean on the other side.

Are you still trying to make yourself clean? What is hindering you from letting go and turning your life completely over to Jesus?

Father, thank You for doing all the dirty work. When I let go and give You control, You take my filthy sin and wash it away. Your payment for my sin on the cross was enough. Help me to rest secure knowing You are in the driver's seat and I am clean.

SELAH
pause in God's presence

_____

_____

_____

_____

_____

_____

TO RISK OR NOT TO RISK

Jesus answered, "If you want to be perfect, go, sell your possessions and give to the poor, and you will have treasure in heaven. Then come, follow me." When the young man heard this, he went away sad, because he had great wealth. Matthew 19:21-22 NIV

"Come," he said. Then Peter got down out of the boat, walked on the water and came toward Jesus. Matthew 14:29 NIV

I often find myself asking God for an open door, guidance, wisdom, a sign, whatever. When I look back at my life, there are specific places I wonder why I never experienced 'Yes' for that season. Now don't misjudge me, I'm fully aware that God often says 'No' or 'Wait' but if I'm truthful, sometimes I play a major role in the outcome. In reality, the door was opened the opportunity given, the dream set in motion, the invitation handed out, but I closed the door on my 'Yes.' I opted for safe because the opposition intensified or the risk seemed too great.

I could have started that business or written that book. I could have made a new friend, taken the class, applied for the job, moved to that city...but I said no. It wasn't God shutting the door, it was me.

The wonderful thing about life is that each one of us has a choice to participate in it. We aren't robots set on a never changing course.

I'm drawn to the story titled the 'Rich Young Ruler' in the Bible. Poor guy, he gets such a bad rap in sermons for choosing money over Jesus. But was that all? It says he was able to honestly answer Jesus that he had kept all the commandments, so obviously, he was faithful and obedient with the choices he had been previously given. As I read his story, I wonder if the risk seemed too great? Sell everything, come, follow me. Leave the security of faithfulness to the law, give up his control and follow a relationship with no sure outcome. Jesus opened the door wide, gave him a 'Yes,' and told him exactly how to get there. He chose to close it.

So many doors I've closed when God offered 'Yes' and yet he still makes good out of my not-best choices. His mercies are new every morning and I get to participate in the trajectory of my life today. I may have given up that chance but He hasn't given up on me.

Have you ever been aware of a time when you said 'No' to God's obvious 'Yes?' What risk is God asking you to take so that you can experience His 'Yes?'

Jesus, I admit I have often allowed control, comfort or fear to convince me to close a door You have opened. Sometimes the chance comes again and sometimes it doesn't. Give me the faith to follow Your lead and take the risk. I want to have eyes to see and a heart that chooses 'Yes' when You open the next door.

SELAH
pause in God's presence

_____

_____

_____

_____

WHOOPSIE

This is the day that the Lord has made; let us rejoice and be glad in it. Psalm 118:24

You make known to me the path of life; in your presence there is fullness of joy; at your right hand are pleasures forevermore. Psalm 16:11 NIV

"We are out of ink for the printer, can you pick some up?"

Such a simple request shot across my screen that I didn't think twice. "Sure," I quickly replied as I loaded two of our boys up in the van. Lunchtime had come and gone as we finished up our monthly service project at a local non-profit in the neighboring town. Knowing we would pass a store on our way out, I quickly ran through my mental shopping list. You know what I'm talking about. All those random things you forgot on your last list but if you happen to be in the store again you should pick them up.

Surprisingly, I had nothing. The world very well might have stopped spinning for a moment.

What I did have was a hungry tummy and two hungry boys about to bite each other's head off. "Perfect," I thought, "We'll run in the grocery side and grab a quick snack."

Now pause, have you ever had a moment where you look back and say 'what was I thinking?' or 'surely I never thought that possible'? Well, I have lots of those moments. We quickly grab a small cart, head into the store and see the dreaded sign:

CLOSED: TEMPORARILY OUT OF ORDER.

The. Worst. Sign. Ever.

Great, I can use the other entrance. The next thought that runs through my mind is a line from our boy's favorite elf cartoon.

Get in, get out, never be noticed.

As we jet down the center aisle toward the needed printer ink, there it stands before us. The snack mountain of doom in the form of big, round barrels filled with puffed cheese balls. I'm utterly convinced the only reason large displays of such items are placed in the way of everything is to derail every mom on a one-item mission. Somehow between my youngest commandeering the basket handle and my oldest still moaning about the closed snack bar sign, our tiny cart and the display collide. *Oh No!* Oh Yes...those barrels bounce. And roll. And clatter all down the aisle. Good thing there are three of us to scatter quickly and throw our bodies in front of the run-away cheese ball containers. (Can I please have a hood on this shirt?) Hurriedly, we gather the barrels, re-stack the display and get our ink in silence.

I usher my still-speechless boys back to the van where we lose all dignity in peels of laughter while reliving the slow-motion avalanche. "I'm sure glad none of those tops popped off!" one says.

"Did you see how far that barrel rolled?" the other cackles.

No dear, I didn't see, but I'm pretty sure the security camera guys did. They probably replayed it a dozen times, and got a much-needed giggle added to their day.

When is the last time you had a big belly laugh?
Remember to enjoy today. Jesus delights in child-like joy.

Lord, the path I took today didn't turn out as expected. You interrupted my serious, task-oriented plans and made it a day to remember. Thank You for the gift of interruptions and laughter. May I rejoice in having breath today.

SELAH
pause in God's presence

GROWING CONTENTMENT

But godliness with contentment is great gain.
1 Timothy 6:6 NIV

But seek first his kingdom and his righteousness,
and all these things will be given to you as well.
Matthew 6:33 NIV

This past weekend, my neighbor called and said he had a few stacks of extra wood that he wanted to give me. Being a veritable wood hoarder, I rushed right over. When I saw the stack of landscape timbers, I couldn't help the happy dance that escaped. I knew exactly where they were going. Transferring the timbers to their new home in my front yard, I immediately began cutting, nailing and lengthening my beloved raised garden bed. It is rustic but wonderful! Thrilled, I walked inside and scratched 'garden add-on' off my prayer want list. Thank you, Lord, for this blessing.

Last night, God's blessing still very fresh on my mind, my family curled up together to watch Fixer Upper. Now there are few things I enjoy more than ice cream, but gardening and the Gaines family are close rivals. (I hear your sigh) The television screen filled with a plan for a garden. Not just any garden but the most elaborate, beautiful, exquisite garden complete with chickens and picnic table and garden house. It was breathtaking and I soaked in every minute before heading to bed.

As I'm here in the kitchen this morning making waffles for my crew, the white index card clipped to the fridge door catches my attention. Each week we post our chores and a character trait on that card. This week it is contentment: being satisfied because God is working everything together for my good and His glory. A scene from last night flashes thru my mind and I'm acutely aware of how sneaky the enemy is, able to use a simple show to steal my joy and excitement over God's evident blessings. The enemy sows such a small seed of discontent into the mix that often I don't realize that it even got planted.

Of course, it's not magazine worthy but my garden is a gift. It feeds my family and provides lots of one-on-one dirt-bonding time with my boys. Each moment I spend tending plants, I can't help but think of the tender way God tends to me. Picking out weeds, pruning off diseased areas and fertilizing places that are blooming.

As I return to waffles, I recognize the weed and pull it out while contentment settles in my soul. It is possible to truly enjoy others' blessings while embracing my own, though they may look very different. In a few weeks spring will come and the memory of that show will fade away, replaced with a new episode or two of some great renovation, but my garden will remain. The sun will come out and I'll put twice as many seeds in the ground thanks to that scrap pile of wood. God is good and He gets the glory...all because I planted contentment.

Have you ever experienced the fruit of discontentment?
Is it worth letting that seed grow?
Where do you want to plant contentment in your life today?

Father, You have given me more than I could ever need, yet often my flesh wants more. Help me see where I have seeds (or trees) of discontentment growing in my life. I can't weed out my heart all on my own. Show me how to pull up these sinful attitudes and plant an attitude of contentment in my life instead.

SELAH
pause in God's presence

_____

_____

_____

_____

_____

_____

_____

_____

_____

_____

_____

_____

_____

_____

_____

WHITE SANDS WIPE-OUT

So we fix our eyes not on what is seen,
but on what is unseen. For what is seen is temporary,
but what is unseen is eternal. 2 Corinthians 4:18 NIV

It's been five days and six National parks, yet the question we've heard daily is 'when will we be at White Sands?' They cannot wait! I must say that behind the surface level of annoyance at answering for the twentieth time, I'm giddy about taking my boys to a childhood memory of mine. At age nine, I flew out for an alone trip with my Mamá in Las Cruces, New Mexico. We traipsed around the region to Alamogordo, Ruidoso, Cloudcroft and White Sands. Twenty-eight years later, I still remember the expanse of sand and the excitement of plummeting down the side of a pure white sand dune.

As we set out from Phoenix, AZ, seven travel-hours loomed ahead of us...plus a time change. Wanting to arrive by 3:00 pm in order to complete their Junior Ranger program and also play; we bypass stops, eat in the van and have a diaper event (use your imagination).

Upon arrival, we are gifted two extra sand sled discs by college kids exiting the park which allows each boy to have their own. What a blessing. White Sands does not disappoint with a breathtaking view, puffy clouded skies, and shimmering mountains surrounding us. Kicking off flip-flops they race to the top, unaware a storm's brewing just over that ridge. As the boys giggle and goof off, dropping down the dune faces, unwanted drops begin to join us. First on the ground, then down their faces. Rain turns to tears as disappointment overshadows our outing.

Seeking shelter becomes our reason to head back to the visitor center, complete their books, pick out badges and wait out the storm. While the temperature drops and the sky grows black, I feel a cold breeze sweep across my heart. This wasn't in the plan.

My husband, Chris, is an expert at making lemonade out of these two lemon hours, so he ushers the boys into the van to video the dramatic lightning strikes surrounding us. New cries of awe fill my ears while we watch the bright white and orange streaks flicker and dance across the sky. God's beauty is still breathtaking. I just needed a different perspective.

Then it happens, a light breaks thru in the distance. Fifteen minutes down the road before us could be our ticket to another adventure. A choice must be made. Stay and sulk or move forward. We choose to set out in pursuit of the unknown.

What we find exceeds expectations. Wet packed sand and plowed ridges, perfect for sledding jumps. Much colder temperatures and wind, perfect for bundling up in our coats. Flips, flops and wipe-outs perfect for belly laughter. And so our storm brought with it a much richer experience of life on the other side. We just had to keep looking for the sun.

How does your perspective need to change today? What would be different if you chose to take a step of faith toward the unseen?

Father, thank You for never leaving me. Even when the storm clouds my vision, You are still shining. Give me a new perspective today and encouragement to keep looking toward Your Son.

MESS

Come to me, all you who are weary and burdened, and I will give you rest. Take my yoke upon you and learn from me, for I am gentle and humble in heart, and you will find rest for your souls. Matthew 11:28-29 NIV

There he lay in a mess of emotion on the hall floor. Guilt and fear of a consequence wrecking his little body. Kneeling in front of him I ask for his hand. The sobbing response is "I don't want a consequence." It had been thirty minutes of back and forth, the tug of war dance between irrational child and a parent desperate to remain calm. Once again I tell him I love him, stand up and return to fixing dinner. From the corner of my eye I see his body worn from the battle. I desperately want to tell him the future, my heart breaking over his distrust, but I can't make his choice. I return to him again, "Give me your hand," I ask.

"No," he replies, "I don't want a consequence."

"I love you son. Do you trust that I love you?"

As he shakes his head no, sorrow floods my soul. Once again, I say I love you, stand and return to dinner. His emotions calm and I return again, kneel, and ask for his hand. From behind him a brotherly voice says "Don't do it, she's mean, she just wants you upset." And the flood begins again.

So is this how God feels when I battle his character? He is love and cannot be other. I hear my Father say 'a consequence is needed, your sin is apparent,' But instead of trusting his love, I battle. In the wake of guilt and the sorrow of my sin, I can't see truth. All I fear is the penalty I deserve as I hear voices around scream 'save yourself, He isn't good.'

Weary, I return to him again. "Look in my eyes," I ask.

But he can't...won't. I see the battle raging inside. "I love you, look at my eyes," I repeat. His head turns but his eyes look away, up, down, around, determined to miss my gaze. "I love you," I remind him and wait. Knowing full well this is a choice he alone must make. Exhausted and worn, he looks up. "Give me your hand," I whisper.

As he timidly reaches out and grasps my hand, I help him up and into my lap. Rocking and reassuring him, his sobs and body calm as he rests in my grace.

The fight was long and brutal; the war of self against obedience. Control verses surrender. It lasted longer than needed and cost him more emotionally than it should have. The punishment his heart endured was greater than any consequence deserved. And I was broken for him, wishing he would have chosen love and trust sooner.

So my Father whispers, 'Trust my love. Correction comes because I love you. There is no condemnation, you are my child.' And I have a choice. Trust Him and surrender to his loving hands or draw my sword, knowing full well battle always leaves unnecessary scars. His lap is ready and his arms are open. Will I give him my hand?

What area of correction are you fighting God over today? Will you give him your hand and let him lead you up and away?

Father, thank You that even in times of correction You meet me with gentleness and compassion. You desire for my heart to trust You fully. Help me to not battle Your discipline and to also embrace Your grace.

SELAH
pause in God's presence

DOORS

"Why are you so angry?" the Lord asked Cain. "Why do you look so dejected? You will be accepted if you do what is right. But if you refuse to do what is right, then watch out! Sin is crouching at the door, eager to control you. But you must subdue it and be its master." Genesis 4:6-7

Set a guard over my mouth, Lord; keep watch over the door of my lips. Do not let my heart be drawn to what is evil so that I take part in wicked deeds along with those who are evildoers; do not let me eat their delicacies. Psalm 141:3-4 NIV

The morning began in utter silence. No wind, no sound, no sun. Just me, my coffee and my Bible. As my soul drank in the pause, I heard Him speak truth. *Why are you up in arms already today?* I had just been reading a devotional about gentleness and self-control, wholeheartedly in agreement with the message, but was convicted that I fail here more often than I like to admit. I try so hard to make life fun, to keep chaos at bay, to hold it all together. More often than not, a boulder comes shattering that glass house, devastating my efforts and I tumble right down with it.

"Ok then, today is going to be different," I whisper as the sun begins to break over the trees.

Now I should have known, should have been prepared. I've been at this parenting and Jesus gig long enough now to know that self-will rarely gets me further than my big toe but I step right into the demands of the day before praying anyway. *A whole lot of coffee and a little bit of Jesus.* Isn't that how it goes?

This morning the family machine begins to run smooth and fast. All gears working and most without squeaks. I'm engaged and attentive: serving, helping, guiding, reminding. I can do this. Then comes the rub. We all have it, the one (or many) things that get right under our skin, bringing our internal temperature from cool to blistering in two seconds flat. I've learned it most likely lies right between our conviction and our personal sin, stepping on toes that are acutely aware of the blisters. My rub is blame: the enemy of intimacy, the opposer of ownership. Lucky day for me: I have a tiny master blamer on the loose.

The nature of the infraction is small but bolstered by his pride, blame comes, cracks the door, and invades my heart and home. I catch myself recalling my devotional, a jumble of something about gentleness and self-control, yet I'm swallowed up whole as my blisters pop. Fully engaged in the war, our friendly fire wounds deep. When the smoke clears, I'm a wreck.

I had heard the truth but didn't apply it. I hadn't made a battle plan for the war that would arise. I had been warned in advance, yet I self-controlled instead of surrendering to Jesus control...and then I blamed my son for it all. Acutely aware of my part, I apologize both to him and to Christ. Sin was at the door and I had let it right in.

Where are you prone to open the door to sin? What guards do you need to set up to protect your heart, mind, or mouth?

Father, Your Word is clear that this life is full of temptations. Daily I get to choose what doors I open in my life. Give me a desire to open the Bible and be drawn to You and not sin. I can't do it on my own. Jesus

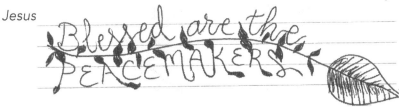

Blessed are the PEACEMAKERS

SELAH
pause in God's presence

THE BICYCLE

If you then, though you are evil, know how to give good gifts to your children, how much more will your Father in heaven give the Holy Spirit to those who ask him!
Luke 11:13 NIV

Every good and perfect gift is from above, coming down from the Father of the heavenly lights, who does not change like shifting shadows. James 1:17 NIV

When my twins turned five, they were finally big enough to get a bicycle. It wasn't that they couldn't ride one sooner, it's just that they were so small and short that only a tricycle fit their legs. Their dad and Poppy braved the Black Friday crazies to snag two blue and red bikes as this extra special Christmas gift. I'm not sure who was more excited, us or them. Knowing for weeks that they had this secret gift tested my poker face to the max. Finally, Christmas arrived and the bikes were revealed. Immediately, their trikes were shoved aside as they straddled the seats and begged to ride and ride. Daddy provided tips and encouragement as they embraced this new adventure. They were determined to learn to use this gift well, pushing each pedal to its full capacity. Off they rode, much farther than they could ride before, while their daddy looked on with pride.

Five years later our struggles are not with fitting on a bike, but with fitting in among peers. Each one of my boys possesses unique and special gifts that make them incredibly special and different. It's like the bicycle among the sea of trikes. As adults, we look on with special insight. We know the gift is so much better than that which is familiar. With a little encouragement, advice and practice, it can take them much further and allow them to see infinitely more than before. But it's a scary thing. Riding away from the familiar on a gift that looks so different from the rest. Learning to work hard, use your gift well and push to your full capacity. And so we encourage and cheer, full of pride when they decide to try again.

"Don't hide your gift," I whisper. "Your Father picked it out especially for you and He can't wait to see you use it."

What gift or talent have you set aside because of fear?
What have you given up on because it requires effort?

Father, You see my uniqueness as a prize to be treasured. Often, I see my differences as hindrances. Give me courage today to use the gifts You picked out especially for me.

SELAH
pause in God's presence

_____

_____

_____

_____

_____

_____

_____

_____

OVERFLOW

A good person produces good things from the treasury of a good heart, and an evil person produces evil things from the treasury of an evil heart. What you say flows from what is in your heart. Luke 6:45

Walking into our hotel breakfast, I spied a state-shaped waffle iron and my heart went pitter-patter. I immediately wanted to check Amazon online and see if it shipped Prime. It's not that we are lacking in the waffle iron area. My cupboard holds a heart shaped iron, a Belgian iron and let's not leave out the very necessary Captain America waffle iron. Is it really necessary to have three waffle irons?

I find myself giddy over waffles, which is partly to blame for our Sunday breakfast-for-dinner routine. With five males in my house, food is a labor of love...and I do mean labor. As all three of those lids open and close on Sunday evenings, I'm reminded that my heart pours love into each mold along with the batter. It is all served up with a side of honey thank-you's and sweet syrup kisses. I'm convinced maybe it is not so bad to have three waffle irons after all. What you have overflowing is just evidence of what you love and for us, on Sunday nights, from the overflow of the heart...the mouth eats.

What is your heart full of today? How do your actions bear evidence of the condition of your heart? Take some time to list out some things that consume your time, money, words and thoughts. Bring it before the Lord and allow Him to speak into those things.

Father, thank You for the truth that the state of my heart can often be seen in the state of my mouth and actions. Correct me and show me where I need to change what fills me up. I want my life to overflow with You.

SELAH
pause in God's presence

_____

_____

_____

_____

_____

_____

_____

_____

_____

_____

_____

_____

_____

_____

_____

_____

DADDY CAN FIX IT

And we know that God causes everything to work together¹ for the good of those who love God and are called according to his purpose for them.
Romans 8:28

'Jack of all trades, master of none.' That saying was a common one I heard as a child and when I grew up I happened to marry one. However, he regularly falls more into the category of 'jack of all trades, master of most.' It's quite handy for me to have such a skilled fixer around the house, but sometimes I wonder about our boys' perception of reality. Just this morning, as I heard some cars and toys crashing to the floor, I reminded the kids that recklessness leads to brokenness.

"But Daddy can fix it," was the quick reply.

Yesterday the rubber chicken broke. "Daddy can fix it with his magic glue."

Last week, Elijah jumped on my footrest. "Sorry Mommy, but Daddy can fix it."

Clogged toilet? Daddy fixed it. Lawnmower issues? Daddy fixed it. Mommy forgot dinner? Daddy fixed that, too. When Luke tripped into the doorway and fractured his finger, I found myself comforting him with, "Don't worry bud, Daddy can fix it."

Sometimes the reality is that the object in question just isn't fixable. However, as a parent, it is such a joy to see the confidence my children have in their daddy. Trust has been built and they have walked through enough life experiences with him that their reflex response is that he will bring about good from the broken circumstance. As I grow older with my Heavenly Father, I long to have the same reflex response. To know, regardless of the circumstance, that my Daddy can fix it.

What do you need your Daddy to fix today?

Daddy, You are the best fixer I know. It seems hopeless but I trust that You can make something good from this mess. Thank You in advance.

_____

_____

_____

_____

_____

_____

_____

_____

_____

_____

_____

PITTER PATTER

I will lie down and sleep in peace, for You alone, O Lord,
make me dwell in safety. Psalm 4:8 NIV

Let your unfailing love surround us, Lord, for our hope
is in you alone. Psalms 33:22

Waking up multiple times a night with kids tests the Jesus in me. Our nights have been rough lately. Between a new potty-trainer and an asthmatic, our chances of getting a full night of sleep is about the same as winning the lottery. Although, I'm pretty sure I would be just as thrilled with sleep as I would money. The last few nights we have added 'I'm scared' to the mix. As the weather flip flops from winter to spring, the 'wind comes sweeping cross the plain' loudly rushing through the trees and whistling around our home. We might not hear the tree that falls in the forest, but we definitely know what caused it.

The pitter-patter of feet comes down the hall and before I open my eyes, I can sense the tiny human staring in my face. Surely, if I don't move, don't open my eyes, he will go back to bed. It's silent for a moment. Then, I feel a warm breath on my nose as a quiet whisper says "I'm scared, will you come sleep with me?"

Exhausted and not wanting to get up, I pull him up in bed and tuck him under my arm. (I would have put him in the middle, but that spot was already occupied by the asthmatic child.) Restless breathing eventually gives way to snores as his body falls limp beside mine. The wind is still howling but it's different now. Fully secure, all fear removed, peace covers him and rest comes.

When my soul is restless, overwhelmed at the sound of life around me, I often find myself awake at night. 'Daddy, I'm scared, anxious, disappointed and confused.' Pick one or add your own. We've all had those thoughts if we have lived any length of time. Sometimes I even feel like I have to tip-toe around the corner. Desperately wanting to be near God but hesitant to wake him up. When I finally whisper, I find don't have to wait for him to open His eyes. He was already sitting up, waiting and welcoming my presence. No other words are needed. Pulled up close to Him, I rest knowing the truth that I am secure in His love. The wind may rush and roar but I have peace and will soundly sleep.

Do you ever find yourself awake and anxious in the dark? What is keeping you from getting up and going to God with your fears?

Father, You are always awake and awaiting my presence. I'm not a bother or a disturbance. The darkness is scary and I really need Your peace. Help me hear Your words of truth and trust Your love.

SELAH
pause in God's presence

_____

_____

_____

_____

_____

_____

TRANSFUSION

The thief comes only to steal and kill and destroy;
I have come that they may have life, and have it to
the full. John 10:10 NIV

For you know that God paid a ransom to save you from
the empty life you inherited from your ancestors. And it
was not paid with mere gold or silver, which lose their
value. It was the precious blood of Christ, the sinless,
spotless Lamb of God. 1 Peter 1:18-19

I love my kids, but having kids does not love me. My body revolts and rebels, leading to months of shots and precautionary medical care. A few years ago, a normal evening turned tragic soon after our fourth baby turned one. While celebrating my grandpa's birthday, I began bleeding uncontrollably and by the time my husband rushed me to the hospital, the situation was critical. Hemorrhaging and losing consciousness, the doctors rushed me into surgery. Imagine our shock, when we were told it was a close call and that I had also miscarried. Overwhelmed by the extreme loss of blood and now the loss of our child, I literally felt drained of the life in me. As the week progressed I could not gain ground, my blood levels steadily dropping and weakness overtaking me.

Concern for my health growing, my doctor suggested a blood transfusion, infusing me with the life-giving blood of another. It's amazing really, to know that someone else could give me back my life, but due to a family incident with tainted blood I was terrified. Weak, irrational and scared, I just couldn't bring myself to trust this option until my husband quietly spoke up. You see my husband, my beloved, is blood-type O. He would be my donor. There was no need to fear. He willingly chose to bleed out as much as they could take into that collection bag, knowing exactly where it was going.

As we sat the next day in the hospital room, the nurse came in with several bags and asked for my consent. I looked for only one thing, *Given by Chris Thomas.* Peace immediately filled my soul as they hung the bags above my head. With each drip his blood began to flow thru my veins, my body accepting the life-giving nutrients it so desperately required.

The Bible says we are all spiritually dying, losing our life from the hemorrhaging effects of sin, and we need a transfusion. Our bodies are not capable of restoring life on their own, but whose blood do we choose? The blood of this world is tainted and diseased, but the blood of Jesus Christ is trustworthy and pure. And He is the lover of our soul. He came and chose to bleed out and give us His life. When you accept His sacrificial gift and allow Him to be your Savior, the anatomy of your life changes. When His life blood flows through your veins and renews you, it replaces everything that wasn't enough to sustain life and instead, you receive abundant life for eternity.

Give thanks today to Jesus for His selfless sacrifice for you.

Jesus, "thank you" doesn't even begin to describe how I feel. I was dying and needed new life and you gave it to me. Just because You love me. Help me to never take for granted the life You sacrificed for me. Because of Your gift, I get to live a full life today.

If you are not sure that Jesus is the leader and savior of your life, read through the following verses or talk with someone about salvation:
Romans 3:23
Romans 6:23
Romans 5:8
Romans 10:9
Romans 10:13
Romans 5:1
Romans 8:1
Romans 8:38-39

SELAH
pause in God's presence

_____

_____

_____

_____

_____

_____

_____

_____

_____

_____

_____

_____

_____

_____

_____

_____

_____

OH, THE DEPTHS

Oh, how great are God's riches and wisdom and knowledge! How impossible it is for us to understand his decisions and his ways!
Romans 11:33

A few years after we had our twins, a dear friend offered to teach my husband, Chris, and I how to scuba dive. Living in the middle of the country, a full day's drive from the nearest ocean, it seemed a strange opportunity but we had learned to not kick gift horses in the mouth.

Words don't even begin to describe how that experience changed us and we began planning a grand celebration for our fifteenth wedding anniversary: diving the Great Barrier Reef off the coast of Australia. We have dear friends who have moved back to the Gold Coast, so making the trip held advantages in more ways than one. After five years of planning, saving and seeking God for timing, we found ourselves waiting to board the Tusa6 dive boat headed out to the Great Barrier Reef...on Chris's birthday no less.

Excitement coursed through my body as I suited up and took that giant step off the boat into the Coral Sea. Chris never has any trouble jumping in and heading straight down, but every time I dive, I panic...just for a minute. You know it is really not natural to breathe underwater. Encouraged by my husband, I regained my composure and began sinking deep below the surface. Five meters, ten meters, twenty meters. The beautiful expanse of the sea floor unfolded before us like a giant tapestry.

We kept an eye on the local guides nearby as blue sea stars, giant clams (that I could have fit inside), exotic fish, and a green sea turtle swam circles around us. For an entire morning we explored ridges and valleys, crevices and coral shelves, yet upon surfacing each time, we found ourselves within earshot of the boat. What we had explored was truly just a drop in the ocean compared to what remained. Drying off on deck during the hour ride back, we saw glimmers of innumerable coral reefs passing just below the surface. They announced their presence yet still hid the full truth of the beauty and extravagance that lay within them.

Our creator God is even more extravagant. Revealing his presence in glimmers and glimpses yet containing unimaginable beauty below the vast surface of what we can see. His world is one of intrigue adventure that would take innumerable lifetimes to explore. Yet He beckons us to jump in, sink deep, and trust him to be our breath as we explore the small drop of our life in the ocean of His plan. He is our ultimate guide, showing how each new turn opens up a world of intricate beauty we could never have found on our own.

For half a day, I got to explore one of the seven wonders of the world, but because I have chosen to pursue Jesus, I get to explore the wonders of my God every day for the rest of my lifetime.

Does thinking about going 'all in' with God make you panic? Where will He want me to go? How will I breathe? Trust Him and jump in. Don't let fear make you miss out on the relationship of a lifetime. He desires to show you His extravagance.

Father, I've just seen glimpses and glimmers of You from the surface. Help me to dive in and sink deep in Your love. You desire to surround me, guide me, and show me parts of your nature that I never dreamed existed. I trust my next breath to You and open my eyes to experience Your beautiful plan for me.

SELAH
pause in God's presence

HE IS *before* ALL THINGS

THE SUN COMES UP

But joyful are those who have the God of Israel as their helper, whose hope is in the Lord their God. Psalm 146:5

For his anger lasts only a moment, but his favor lasts a lifetime! Weeping may last through the night, but joy comes with the morning. Psalm 30:5

The sun rises at one end of the heavens and follows its course to the other end. Nothing can hide from its heat. Psalm 19:6

In the midst of the silence I hear a shuffle around my bed followed by "Mommy, I need you."

Groggily I stir and get up to take his hand and walk back to bed. "What's wrong?" I question.

"I had a mean dream and was scared," his small voice quivers.

We stop to pray and ask Jesus to restore peace and rest over his heart and mind. Usually he hops straight back to bed but tonight he lingers and turns for a hug.

"I love you a whole bunch mommy...I can't wait for the sun to come up."

"Oh buddy, when night is over the sun always comes up."

His mind at ease, he bounds back to bed as I shuffle back to mine, my mind racing with the truth spoken right then to the midst of my soul.

Darkness hides so much stuff. It pretends things it's not, grows fear, and feels ongoing. It often drags on and tries to occupy my mind for longer than necessary. Praise be to the Lord of hope, the Son of God, who never sleeps or grows weary. He sets the heavens in order and reveals his hand as the sun rises on each new day. I'm always in awe of the sunrise, and maybe it is because with the first break of light the memory of night is gone. A new day awaits, the promise of life, and I can't help but smile and take a deep breath.

The night might be scary and seems like it will last forever but joy is coming with the sun in the morning.

Do you feel lost and alone in the dark? Do you stay scared in bed, or get up and go find your Father? Pray for the Lord to renew the truth that morning is coming.

Jesus, You never sleep or turn away from me. I'm always on Your mind and Your heart beats right along with mine. This season feels dark and scary. Hold my hand and lead me into Your peace. Remind me again that morning always comes after the night.

SELAH
pause in God's presence

_____

_____

_____

_____

_____

STILL SMALL VOICE

Whether you turn to the right or to the left,
your ears will hear a voice behind you, saying,
"This is the way; walk in it." Isaiah 30:21 NIV

Yesterday was full. I've been embracing more margin in my days, so when I see a list of to-do's stacked together on one day it kind of makes my insides cringe. They were all good things: Bible study, monthly lunch date, deliver a meal to a friend, school open house and our weekly family night. I had my timeline set, kids loaded up and we headed down the road...twice actually, well to be honest, it should have been three times because I still forgot my grocery list, but twice late was enough already. During our drive to school, I quickly ran through our morning routine with the kids: gifts song, family cheer & our character trait for this week...obedience.

Obedience: doing what you're asked, right away, with a willing attitude. Get it, got it, go.

Ending lunch, I set off to check the rest of the list. Needing to stop by the store to grab bread to go with the dinner I was delivering, I run through a mental list of 'what else should I bring?' (note the forgotten list above). Maybe some snacks for the kids, some chips or drinks, and just like that comes *bring them a box of diapers*. What? Diapers have nothing to do with food. Back I go to considering snack options as I walk in the store...on the health and beauty side no less. (I really have a problem of not entering stores on the side I actually need to be on). *Go buy a box of diapers.* It is so loud, so overwhelming and so NOT snack related that I can't ignore it. After all, I did just quiz the kids on the definition of obedience. Grabbing diapers and bread, I check out and drive on.

Arriving and unloading, I ring the doorbell. Food bag in one hand and diapers in the other, still confused by my recent purchase. When my friend opens the door, my awkward greeting is "Hi, I brought food...and a box of diapers...umm not sure if you need these."

Now you would have thought I brought a lottery check. Grabbing the diapers and hugging them she tells me all about how she couldn't stop at the store after the doctor appointment because their special needs kids were in crisis and needed to get home and that they only have two diapers left. I couldn't do anything but smile and hug her.

Jesus loves her family extravagantly, and let me in on just how much today. Thank you, Jesus, for ears to hear in the midst of 'busy' and for the obedience lesson this morning that helped me follow Your lead.

What act of obedience is God waiting on you to complete?
Are you listening for His voice today?

Father, thank You that You promise to lead me in both the little and big things in life. Help me recognize Your voice today.

SELAH
pause in God's presence

_____

_____

_____

_____

_____

JUST A LITTLE BIT MORE

Now all glory to God, who is able, through his mighty power at work within us, to accomplish infinitely more than we might ask or think.
Ephesians 3:20

If you are faithful in little things, you will be faithful in large ones. But if you are dishonest in little things, you won't be honest with greater responsibilities. Luke 16:10

I'm a dream big, settle small kind of person. Grand ideas but I talk myself out of them really quickly. I label myself 'practical' and say I'm content with what I have. I make a really good case for why it's better to happily live in the 'less than.' Really it's a faith issue.

The major hiccup is I am really faithful in the small things. I've proven myself to act wisely and make good decisions with the measure I've been given. It's the big stuff where I don't trust myself. What if I mess up? Can't handle it? What if it's too much? What if I damage God's name or my witness? I'd rather stay in my small comfort zone where I have faith that He (and I) can keep it together than test my faith in a big God that wants to trust me with more.

The Bible says that when I am faithful in the little things, he wants to make me faithful with much. Stop and reread Ephesians 3:20. It's His power at work in me and you have to admit, God doesn't have an inability problem. Sure, my 'fear of failure' self is terrified but I'm continually drawn to dream about His exceedingly and abundantly more promise. I'm not talking about more house, car or money here, instead it's the what-ifs that I can't even fathom. Parts of me that haven't even been put into motion. What if my life is designed to give more? Invest more? Impact more? Love more?

I don't look at my kids and see sitting and breathing as an abundant life. I rejoice when they use their gifts, embrace training, prove themselves faithful and take on new responsibilities. We delight in giving them more and, at this current stage of life, with eager open hands they will take all we give out. Could it be that God looks at me the same way? He has seen my faithfulness and is excitedly handing over more along with a huge dose of His ability.

I'm not in denial that I have all the head knowledge of what I should do yet I still struggle to actually take that first step. Instead, I need to trust that He knows what He is doing when I'm given something bigger. Ultimately it's my choice: be content to keep my faith small or test my faith, trust God and dream big.

Do you tend to settle for small or instead do you dream big? Could God be asking you to trust His choice to do more through you? Name one area you would like to expand your faithfulness this month.

Father, You keep asking more of me and I'm scared that I can't handle it. Forgive me for making excuses to not let You work through me. I know Your plans are beyond my comprehension and I want to be faithful. May my little step of faith today lead to a greater step of faith tomorrow.

SELAH
pause in God's presence

_____

_____

_____

_____

_____

_____

_____

_____

_____

_____

_____

_____

_____

_____

_____

_____

_____

SURF LIFESAVER

And he said to the human race, "The fear of the Lord—
that is wisdom, and to shun evil is understanding."
Job 28:28 NIV

Jesus told him, "I am the way, the truth, and the life.
No one can come to the Father except through me."
John 14:6

Beginning on our honeymoon, Chris and I decided to dream big, save and plan for our special anniversaries. We believe every five years completed in marriage is a huge, miracle worth celebrating. Year five was a trip to Disney World (no kids yet and wonderful, minus a small fight over the dropped camera). Year ten, we ventured to Cozumel for a scuba trip and during the flight home Chris leaned over and said "15, Great Barrier Reef, Australia."

"YES!" was my immediate response. Little did I know, we were currently adding a new man to our mix and another would come along as well. Several years passed and with four kids underfoot and life responsibilities, would that trip ever happen now? God is faithful and our trip-planning diligence was rewarded five years later with just one major change order... bring the big boys with us.

Now you can imagine what a big difference it is between ocean coast and the plains of Oklahoma. We have a small pond at home and we have boated on lakes. I have even taken the boys to the brown waters of the Gulf of Mexico coast near my Louisiana hometown, but standing where wild ocean meets land just takes your breath away. The boys were terrified of the roar.

Because we stayed with dear friends who have intimate knowledge of that oceanfront, Chris and I willingly let Miles and his four boys take over as teachers. They showed our sons how to jump and duck under waves, body surf and boogie board, but most importantly they taught them about riptides and what the surf safety flags meant.

The trained surf lifesavers set flags along the beach to keep you swimming in water safe from riptides and danger. Their diligent watch from above often requires moving the flags up and down along the stretch of sand. It's your job to make sure you swim between the flags. After a week of ocean swimming, their fear was washed out to sea. My boys were all in. Saltwater now ran through their blood.

As I stood on the beach that final evening making sure all the boys stayed between the flags, Luke came towards me with a huge smile on his face. "I love the ocean, it is so much fun!" he exclaimed as he ran by.

"Yes, but it is also dangerous," I called after him.

His small frame stopped and turned toward me. "Just like God," he replied on his way to jump back in.

Yes son, just like God…and with that I'm again reminded of truth. When I stay within the safety of His boundary flags, my God is love and joy and fills my soul with excitement. Outside of that protection, He is extremely dangerous, powerful and fierce. My strength against His current of justice will fail every time, yet Jesus is my life saver. He marks the way to the deep waters of grace where I can laugh with all that is within me as I allow His love to wash over me.

Do you see God as fun or fear?
What would it take for you to find the fun in respecting His power? Do you trust that Jesus alone can save you?

Father, You set the world in motion and the tides rise and fall at Your command. You are powerful and mighty, able to move anything and anyone at anytime. Yet, You want me to have an intimate knowledge of You and find comfort in Your power. Thank You for sending Jesus to mark the way. Through Him, I experience Your mighty power in the most loving way.

SELAH
pause in God's presence

RESTLESS

I am not saying this because I am in need, for I have learned to be content whatever the circumstances. I know what it is to be in need, and I know what it is to have plenty. I have learned the secret of being content in any and every situation, whether well fed or hungry, whether living in plenty or in want. I can do all this through him who gives me strength. Philippians 4:11-13 NIV

It's January and the weather has been crystal clear. As I sit here at the table looking out on my porch swing, it beckons me to come. The sun is shining, the wind is still, the scenic view from inside looking out is perfect. However, all is not as it seems. The harsh, chilling reality of below freezing temperatures convinces me it's better to stay put inside. Oh, but inside is rough today. Tension runs high as we have been on cold weather house arrest for days. Stir crazy and unable to escape, there are only so many games of Candyland and Match a mom can play. I'm restless and just want out. If I'm honest, this isn't the only time the pressures of life have made me want to run away and seek a different circumstance.

In the restlessness, God calls me to stop and rest. I truly do have all I need. Food, clothes and shelter. My healthy kids, a Bible, and five cups of hot chocolate. It's my soul, not the circumstances, that needs a change. I've started functioning in my own strength and in turn, I lost my contentment along the way. Caught up in the monotony of what my eyes see, I'm restless and want a different view.

Paul reminds me in Philippians that contentment is a learned choice. However, it comes not through my own ability but through Christ's ability alone. I have to do life through him and his way.

"Jesus, show me how to do life your way today," I whisper.

Standing up and turning, I take one last glance at the swing and notice its shadow. Silently I'm reminded that the sun is still present even in the midst of winter. The same goes for God. No matter what season of life I am in, He is present and able to give me the strength I need to be content.

Do you ever want to run away from your current situation? Where do you need God to strengthen you so you can be content?

Father, if I'm really honest, there are times I just want to run away from the trials of life. When I use my own strength, I take credit for the good times and complain in the hard times. I want to learn to rest in all seasons knowing You are strong enough to handle every situation.

SELAH
pause in God's presence

_____

_____

_____

_____

_____

BRIDGE THE GAP

Each of you should use whatever gift you have received to serve others, as faithful stewards of God's grace in its various forms. 1 Peter 4:10 NIV

We have a few acres of land behind our house but a creek has cut a deep, wide gorge between them. Now, if I had the agility of a deer or a spring like Tigger, there wouldn't be a problem getting across. Instead, my refurbished knees let me know exactly what they think of every step down and back up to the other side. The boys don't mind the trek so much until the fallen leaves in autumn form a deceptive bottom. One wrong step and they are immediately waist deep in leaves scrambling to get out. We really need a bridge, but fifty foot logs aren't just lying around you know.

Fortunately for us, a recent windstorm felled quite a few smaller trees and limbs near the creek. With their eyes on the prize, all the boys set to work gathering, sorting and dragging branches of varying sizes into a bridge halfway down the inside of the gorge. We even moved a large tree trunk together over and in for a handrail. Joy beamed from their bodies and encouragement spilled from their mouths as they bounced back and forth across the creek on their newly constructed bridge. No more surprise steps.

For a moment that day, I got to watch an amazing team. Four vastly different individuals, each using their gifts for the benefit of another. Setting aside their pecking order and pride in favor of a common goal. How full my mom heart felt. I know that's what God is speaking to me these days. He longs to look over with pride at His family's teamwork. Many different gifts and parts working together to bridge the gap.

How can you use your gifts today to serve those around you?

Father, give me a heart of teamwork and the desire to use my gifts to serve others. I know we can do more together than we can apart.

_____

_____

_____

_____

_____

_____

_____

_____

_____

_____

_____

_____

THE CLOUDY VEIL

For now we see only a reflection as in a mirror; then we shall see face to face. Now I know in part; then I shall know fully, even as I am fully known.
1 Corinthians 13:12 NIV

But whenever someone turns to the Lord, the veil is taken away. For the Lord is the Spirit, and wherever the Spirit of the Lord is, there is freedom. So all of us who have had that veil removed can see and reflect the glory of the Lord. And the Lord—who is the Spirit—makes us more and more like him as we are changed into his glorious image.
2 Corinthians 3:16-18

An hour south through the winding mountain roads brings us over the ridge to Asheville, North Carolina. I've read for years about this quaint little town nestled in the Blue Ridge Mountains and my eyes are finally feasting on its beauty. After a quick check-in to a hotel room with a shower. Praise! Because living with 5 males in a tent for days makes the stink overwhelming. We grab food and race the sunset to the heralded best-lookout view around, Craggy Dome Pinnacle and overlook.

The Blue Ridge Parkway lives up to its name of America's most beautiful highway as we ascend through tunnels and over small ridges climbing in elevation. Mount Mitchell in the distance reaches into the clouds while clear skies and vistas provide 'ooh and ahh' views around each bend.

Higher we drive until the Craggy Ridge sweeps us right up into the approaching clouds. I've never been in a cloud outside of a plane, so the swirling fluff around me and dropping temperature takes away my breath.

We park and hike 3/4 of a mile to the peak amid rhododendron trees arching, twisting and folding themselves around the well traveled path. It's apparent this site is desirable for memorable events as pretty girls in flowing dresses smile adoringly for photographers. They are all waiting for the perfect moment to capture greatness; however, my view ends five feet ahead.

It's such a disappointment. We had made a plan, hiked the trail and have absolutely nothing to see for it now as our eyes scan the misty gray wall. Blinded by the all-encompassing cloud, I stand in stillness huddled against my oldest son. It's cold, windy and silent as my heart wrestles with its longing for a magazine-worthy view and the dreamy experience I had envisioned. After what seems to be an eternity of waiting, we turn to leave because I hear my third son saying over and over, "I want to go, I can't see anything."

Dejected, I step but then glimpse a ray and choose to stay instead. I'm awestruck as the wind blows a hole through the cloud and suddenly I get to drink in the view. The curtain cloud rolls aside to reveal ridge after ridge fading away in ombré hues of blue and gray. Rays of sunlight shine down reflecting off the saturated sky. The mist and clouds provide depth and interest in the peaks and valleys that you can almost hear singing praises to God. *Behold His glorious workmanship. For now we see in part but then we shall see in whole.*

Hand in hand, my son and I squeal with glee during our moments of gazing. As quickly as it opened, the clouds sweep back in and obscure what lies beyond, but I am no longer disappointed. Instead, I'm reminded that what we often want in life is the sunshine sky with no cloud in sight. The picture perfect view to adore and capture for the story of our life while we run from mountain top to mountain top.

What we find instead, while standing in the clouds, is time to rest and breathe, to look around and wait for the light when its sudden breakthrough will reveal sights we longed to see and hoped to find. The clouds give depth and interest to places we would have otherwise overlooked and provide a reflecting point for God to gloriously shine.

In the midst of the cloud, His presence envelopes us and His quiet voice is wrapped up in the intimacy of leading us while we see only a few steps ahead. And as we wait with Him hand in hand, He also delights with us when the view opens up for miles. Although I may not see it now, the truth remains...His majesty is still very present, just beyond the veil.

What having you been hoping to see and haven't yet? Linger a little longer and acknowledge that His glory is still present.

Father, when the gray nothingness surrounds me, let not my heart be troubled. No matter what lies seek to blind me, the truth remains. You are here. Your glory is real and present. Shine through and give me a glimpse of your presence today.

_____

_____

_____

_____

_____

HE WHO began {a} good work IN YOU will bring it {to} completion

ACKNOWLEDGEMENTS

Thank you to the YouVersion team for providing a platform where I learned how to write. Without you, this book would never exist.

To my many friends who gave me advice and encouraged me that I had a story to share even when I was scared.

To my dear friend Denee – your listening ear and ever-present smile bless me.

To my sister-in-laws – my cheerleaders. Your constant prodding and questions about progress kept me going.

To my mom – the best storyteller I know. Thank you for planting the seed to find the silver lining in everything. We're making memories.

To my boys – this is our story. You sharpen me daily and help me find Jesus. What a blessing it is to be your momma.

To Chris – you saw this diamond in the rough and still make me feel wonderfully chosen. What a beautiful journey we walk hand in hand. Your dedication to the Lord and leadership of our family makes it easy to follow. I'm so glad you were not what I thought I wanted, but instead exactly what I needed.

To Jesus – You are my everything. I deserve nothing yet You have entrusted this beautiful mess to me. What amazing grace I've found!

ABOUT THE AUTHOR

Shauna Thomas understands the pressures of both working and stay-at-home mothers. After many years of parenting four boys while working full-time in ministry, she now works full time managing her family at home. She enjoys painting, drawing, fishing and digging in her garden. One day she hopes to have chickens but for now her roost is full. She has been married to her husband, Chris, for 18 years, lived in four states and they currently reside outside of Edmond, Oklahoma. Her life story is so full of twists and turns that friends used to say 'you should write a book about it.' So she did.

More stories from Shauna Thomas and The Shadow of My Porch Swing are available as devotional plans on YouVersion, the free Bible app, or online at www.familyunite.org.

WRITE YOUR STORY

Made in the USA
Lexington, KY
23 July 2019